BLUE MOUNTAINS
WILDERNESS

PANOSCAPES

PETER LIK

WILDERNESS PRESS

"My total dedication and obsession with photography has taken me on journeys into many remarkable areas throughout Australia. I captured this collection of "Panoscapes" using a specialist panoramic camera. Because of the wider field of view, this format enables me to portray the true spirit of Australia on film. Upon viewing these images I am sure you will share with me the tranquillity and solitude I experienced whilst capturing the stunning beauty of this country."

Front cover - Three Sisters, Blue Mountains
Back cover - Autumn colours
Title Page - Upper Wentworth Falls

ISBN 0 9587002 9 X

© Wilderness Press 2000 BK10

Reprinted 1998, 2000

® Panoscapes is a registered trademark of Peter Lik's Wilderness Press Pty Ltd.
Published by Wilderness Press, an imprint of Peter Lik's Wilderness Press Pty Ltd
PO Box 2529 Cairns Queensland 4870 Australia
Telephone (07) 4032 1266 Facsimile (07) 4032 1277
Email info@peterlik.com.au
To my Sister Di

www.peterlik.com

Peter Lik's
WILDERNESS PRESS
Pty Ltd

Rising from the coastal plain 65 kilometres west of Sydney, the Blue Mountains offer spectacular scenery to its millions of visitors every year. Formed over 200 million years ago, the entire area lay under a sea bed. Over time, sandstone formed and movement in the earths crust gradually forced this gigantic plateau to where it is today. Often shrouded in clouds or surrounded by swirling mist, the magnificent sentinels of the Three Sisters, Echo Point, Katoomba are the highlight of this magnificent region. The panoramic Blue Mountains National Park covers 216,000 hectares and is the fourth largest national park in the state.

The City of the Blue Mountains has over 20 towns and villages. Place such as Katoomba, Blackheath, Leura, Wentworth Falls and Glenbrook provide cosy, old style guesthouses where you can enjoy an open log fire and relax after a days exploring.

Hiking in the Blue Mountains can take you on short strolls or overnight hikes for the more serious. Bush walking takes you through valleys, delightful rainforest glens such as the Grand Canyon and past many of the superb waterfalls in the Blue Mountains where you can really feel the majesty of the mountains. Many lookouts provide panoramic views of this impressive region with some gorges plunging 600 metres in to the valleys below.

With the constantly changing weather and light conditions, the escarpments change their moods; glowing with afternoon sun, shimmering under a rain shower or cradled in mist which makes it a photographer's paradise. The "blueness" of the Blue Mountains is caused by the eucalypt (gum) trees dispersing fine droplets of oil into the atmosphere which cause the blue light rays of the sun to be scattered more effectively.

The Three Sisters glowing at sunset, Echo Point, Katoomba

Overleaf: Grand Canyon - stairway to heaven

Crystal clear skies over Narrowneck

Rosedale Cottage

Cosy guest house, Blackheath

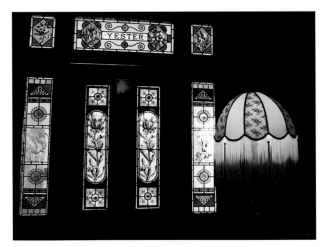

Classic leadlighting at Yester Grange

A charming old pub, Megalong Valley

The colours of autumn

Golden poplars

Fiery autumn leaves

Old fashioned lace framed in the window of a stone cottage

Leura gardens

A classic dry stone wall in the Blue Mountains

Panormic vista from Govetts Leap towards Lycon Plateau

Overleaf: Magnificent Katoomba Falls

Mountain mist cascades over the Three Sisters and Jamison Valley

Early morning Gods rays, Katoomba

Sunrise illuminates a lone tree enveloped in fog, Leura

King ferns flourish in the Jamison Valley

Wild skies at Echo Point

Sun highlights the Three Sisters

Stunning clouds over Kanangra Walls

Pastel hues over the Three Sisters

Classic shack in Megalong Valley

Time stood still in this farmers shack, complete with a classic FJ Holden ute.

Sundrenched stock yards, Megalong Valley

Magical colours of the Blue Mountains

Pastel flowers, Leura gardens.

View of Katoomba township nestled in the Blue Mountains

Grand architecture of Yester Grange homestead

Terrace Falls cascades over thirteen tiers

Terrace Falls

Cataract Falls

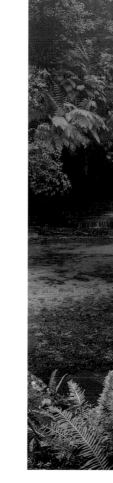

Blackheath Glen

Overleaf: Sundown over a rustic cabin, Megalong Valley

Wildflowers bloom in Jenolan State Forest

Sunset casts its warm glow over the Three Sisters

Rockclimbers ascend Middle Sister

Twilight over Govetts Leap

Sparkling rock pool, Blackheath

Colourful vegetation beneath mountain falls

Overleaf: Majestic Upper Wentworth Falls

Mist shrouds the magical waters of Fairy Falls

Exquisite limestone formation at Jenolan Caves

Caves House at Jenolan Caves provides intimate rooms in a charming guest house

Skyway at the Three Sisters.

Overleaf: Crystal Creek at Kanangra Walls

The Katoomba Scenic Skyway provides magnificent views of the Blue Mountains.

Gods rays over Jamison Valley

An eagle glides the mountains

Hanging rock projects from the walls of Grose Valley

Ancient king ferns at Blackheath Glen

Overleaf: Panoramic vista from Narrowneck Lookout

Katoomba Falls delicately cascade into a mossy garden

Katoomba Scenic Rail - the world's steepest

King ferns

Overleaf: Misty forest in the Blue Mountains

Early morning skies from Narrowneck lookout

Lone Shack

Sunflowers

Millaa Millaa Falls

Great Barrier Reef

Twelve Apostles

Books by Peter Lik

- Australia
- Blue Mountains
- Brisbane
- Cairns
- Daintree and Cape Tribulation
- Fraser Island
- Gold Coast
- Great Barrier Reef
- Port Douglas
- Sunshine Coast
- Sydney
- The Red Centre
- Townsville and Magnetic Island
- Wildlife
- World Heritage Rainforest
- COLLECTORS EDITION
  "Australia - Images of a Timeless Land"
  (Large format 192 page coffee table book)

Peter Lik's
WILDERNESS PRESS
Pty Ltd